Made with ❤ on the BookLeaf Publishing Platform
www.bookleafpub.in
www.bookleafpub.com

The Whispers Within

Navyaa Mutneja

India | USA | UK

Dedication

To those who see beauty in the short and precious moments, and know that everything is connected in one way or the other...

Preface

"I used to think that I was just a messy, imperfect teenager, trying to figure things out. But then, I discovered the whispers within. It's my soul, telling me that I'm strong, capable, and loved.
I've always loved reading, though my brief stint in a book club didn't align with my preference for independent reading choices. I craved the freedom to explore books that resonated with me personally. This love for reading naturally transitioned into a desire to write – be it rhymes, paragraphs, or poems. Writing became an outlet for my emotions, particularly as an introvert who often felt misunderstood when expressing myself verbally.
During challenging times, writing proved to be an invaluable lifeline. The act of fingers to keyboard, provided a safe haven for me to process my emotions, from grief and anger to confusion. It allowed me to unravel the complexities of my experiences and give voice to the feelings that remained unspoken.
In the solitude of writing, I found solace. It became a means of releasing pent-up emotions and gaining a deeper understanding of myself. By exploring my thoughts and behaviors on paper, I discovered hidden patterns and gained a clearer perspective on life's events.

Writing empowered me to reclaim my sense of self and navigate the complexities of my emotions with greater clarity and confidence.

Acknowledgements

I want to thank my massi, Dr Aninda Sidana, you read my poems, you listened to me when I talked about them, and you even told me to try to get them published. This made me feel really happy and encouraged. It means a lot to me that you thought my poems are good and that other people might like them too. Thank you for believing in me, I love you !

Thank you to my mother, Dr Ruchi Sidana, for believing in me, for supporting me when I didn't even want to support myself, for helping me through everything and for being there for me, every time, from when I needed a shoulder to cry to when I needed a best friend to gossip with, I love you !

Thank you to my father, Dr Vikram Mutneja, for supporting me, for loving me even when I didn't even love myself, for having faith in me even when I didn't have faith in myself, I love you !

Thank you to my sister, Naysha, for being my person in the family and keeping my secrets, for being the person who I can talk to, and for being my partner in crime, my baby sister, I love you !

To my dearest friends, Pekhat, Saachi, Samev, Harman, Praneet, Susan, Raavya and many more, I am incredibly grateful for each and every one of you. I cherish the memories we've made together and deeply appreciate the unwavering support you've shown me throughout my journey. You've always believed in me, listened patiently to my ramblings, and stood by me even during my darkest moments when I struggled with self-doubt. I love you all dearly, and while I haven't named everyone individually, please know that my love and gratitude extend to each and every one of you.

Last but not least thank you to all of you, hope you enjoy this book and I'm very grateful that you chose to read this book and to each and every one of you, I love you !

Just a girl

I'm not a poet, no wordsmith blessed,
Just a girl, with a heart that beats a little faster.
Figuring things out, emotions unaddressed,
Learning the language of feelings, a brand new master.
Trying to live, to breathe, to simply be,
Navigating this world, uncertain and free.
So don't mistake me, for someone profound,
I'm just a girl, on familiar ground.

2. Value of toil

The sweetest fruits demand our toil,
True bonds of heart require our soul.
Even paradise, a final cost,
For entrance, earthly life is lost.
Yet in the trade, a truth unfolds,
Eternal light for fleeting gold.

3. The echoed doubt

"I love you" said my bestfriend,
Those words left her mouth,
My mind wandered out,
The voice in my head awoke,
As it spoke,
How could she love you,
How could she love such a mess,
How could she love such a menace,
How could she love such a messed up person,
How could she love you when you are the way you are,
How could she love you when you yourself don't love
you...?

4. Existence and oblivion

Does the loss of a single grain of sand
From a boundless, shifting shore
Truly matter in the grand design,
Where waves forevermore
Wash over, erasing all trace?

Does the ocean weep
When a solitary drop
Dissolves into the deep,
Lost within the endless scope
Of its ever-moving keep?

A leaf descends, a fragile thing,
From branches reaching high,
Lost to the wind's relentless swing,
A whisper in the passing sky,
A fleeting, autumnal sigh.

And what of life, a fragile bloom,
A spark within the vast unknown,

Does its extinguishing consume
The universe, or leave it grown
Indifferent, cold, and alone?

5. Chamber of doubt

Unheard voices,

Unanswered questions,

The why's and the who's,

The where's, the when's,

Till I feel the need to grab my hair and tear it all out,

I just ask myself the same questions,

How do I get this voice in my head to shut up for once,

How do I get these word in my mind to stop hurting for

once,

How do I stop the broken, shattered pieces of my soul to

stop piercing for once,

How do I stop overthinking for once,

How do I not mess it up for once,

How do I get it right just once,

God why do I always mess it up,

Why can't I ever do it right,

Why can't I....?

6. Solitude's Paradox

I'm always lonely,
Doesn't matter if I have people around,
Or if I have no one around,
I'm always lonely,
But despite that I've always had myself to keep me
company,
But last night when I broke down into tears no one
comforted me no helped,
Then I thought,
I'm always lonely,
I cry alone I break alone I shatter alone, tear my soul
alone,
Hell, I even break myself on my own,
I broke my heart by myself and placed it back together
myself,
Then I heard a ghost, or something say,
I'm always lonely,
Not alone,
But always lonely...

7. Fictional forever

Forever ain't possible in real life,
Only fiction knows forever,
When can I get my fictional forever,
Never could I ever stop wondering,
That question never left my head,
and in all the unanswered ones it led...

8. Silent scream

The soul had died,
It was killed,
Minor inconveniences occured,
Major issues made,
The happy little cheerful girl left,
And in her place came the lonely disappointment,
All saw them switch,
No one cried,
They never even bothered to say goodbye,
Seeing her shatter break and scream,
Cry till her demons swallowed her whole,
No one gave a damn,
Everyone just ignored her and left,
She wasn't liked nor was she loved,
She was just a soul roaming with no purpose, no aim, no
care,
Just waiting to say goodbye and leave the whole world
soon,
She could never do so though,
That's how she was,

She was a people pleaser,
Caring about them despite being hated and left alone,
Giving a damn about their opinions despite what they'd
done to her,
She tried to stop but she never could,
Her obvious emotions always blocked the path that she
always soothed.

9. Dust and ashes

Can you make a doll out of dust,
Can you fix a broken doll and make it as good as new,
Can you make a piece of paper with ash,
Can you cut up a piece of paper and make it as good as
new,
Can you ever do so...?

10. Dance of doubt and despair

I cry a lot,
Was it right,
How could I see,
Was it wrong,
Didn't feel like it could be,
But anyways,
Who was I to know,
When I'd never been told so,
But every time I cried,
It felt like I'd done something right,
When I crush and break infront of me,
It's like a reminder to my heart,
That no one will ever stay,
And all I have is myself at the end of the day,
That should be enough for me but it isn't,
I want someone to hold my soul,
Just for a while,
Someone to see my broken ghouls and still love me as if I
am whole,

But if someone ever see's my broken soul,
They'd leave me as if I was never whole...
13

11. Unfinished painting

I draw,
Draw and draw,
But never get to the painting part,
Never get to the way they colour,
Never get the way,
Once I almost got to the painting part,
But turns out I lost all the colours,
Not only the colours but I also lost my paintbrush,
Where could it have been,
Where could I find it...??
Because in it's place nothing else could fit,
I tried every bit,
Got every piece,
Out of this kit,
Nothing I knew of worked like it...

12. Drowning

The knight was going to drown,
But this soon it never knew,
It knew it was going lose,
But this way it never felt,
Because instead of water it
drowned in a sky full of clouds...

13. Silent panic

When I panicked it was silent,
Unlike the others who always went violent,
I looked like I was all calm and packed,
While all everyone saw was the calm and
cool breeze on top,
No one had ever seen the storm in side in
the shop where when I went silent everything
took a stop,
My heart raced faster than anything,
My mind went lost in search of something,
And my soul would loose everything,
All that would ever be left would always be
the outer shell, of calm, packed and collected,
So as I said when I panicked it was silent,
Unlike the others who went violent...

14. Winter's embrace

I always loved winter,
There was something fascinating about it,
About watching the leaves fall from the trees,
Watching the grass loose it's shade,
Watching everything around slowly loose it's jade,
That was beautiful,
It was true beauty,
It was something to be admired,
Well it wasn't admired by all,
Some people ever cursed the beginning of fall,
But to me it was everything,
The beauty of this was indescribable,
Intangible,
It was what I saw myself as,
A beauty that had died,
The beauty of dying a silent yet peaceful and lonely
death,
That was admirable...

15. Bleeding roses

I wish you roses,
A symphony of scent, a vibrant hue,
But all you feel are the thorns,
Sharp and unforgiving, piercing through.
I describe the petals, soft and sweet,
I show you the leaves, a verdant embrace,
I beg you to see the beauty complete,
Yet your gaze remains fixed on the thorns' disgrace.
I offer my last rose, a fragile bloom,
A final plea for you to let go of the gloom.
But still, the thorns, your focus they consume.
And in that moment, a chilling truth I see,
I wished you roses, but you chose to bleed.

16. Paradox of perfection

Was it just my fate,
Or an elder sister's state,
To be loved less,
To be compared, a constant stress,
To live life in a gilded cage,
Or a shadowed, lonely stage?
In my parents' eyes, a perfect pose,
The "good child," bearing life's hard blows.
To always forgive, to quickly mend,
The "bigger person," till the bitter end.
But how long could this burden last?
How long could forgiveness ever cast
A shadow over feelings deep?
How long pretend that I could sleep
While emotions raged within?
If no one sees the storm within,
Guess we'll never truly know
The weight of this invisible woe.

17. Healing embrace

The soft warm feeling it gave,
The way it felt as if it could heal,
As if it could make me feel,
As if it could mend my broken heart,
And make it into art,
Well that's how it felt when you were happy,
Like a warm blanket in winter,
That feeling when you come home from a cold day in
winter,
And in your blanket you go,
With a cup of tea,
Nothing could beat it,
None of yall,
And neither the coming of fall...

18. My ride or die

"She's just a friend", said someone,
"She's just a person", said another someone,
"She's gonna leave you soon" said one I disliked,
I glared at them in my woke as I spoke,
She's not just a girl,
To all she may be no one,
But to me she's the one,
To me she's the prettiest I've ever seen, an ethereal
beauty on earth,
To me she's the one on whom I lean,
To me she's the one who gives the best advice,
And to me she's more than she ever thought she could
be.
I may not have know her long,
Probably only a few months or sometime through,
But stating the facts I know from this point on,
She'll be me my ride or die for today and long on...

19. Beyond exterior

"Never judge a book by its cover."
I never truly believed it, not until now,
When I realized they were right somehow,
This tall figure,
May seem intimidating, a daunting sight to some,
But beneath that exterior, a golden heart resides,
A gentle soul, a beacon in the night.
She might appear fierce, ready to tear you apart,
But instead, she'll mend your broken, weary heart.
She'll piece you back together, soul and all,
And never leave you, not until the final curtain call.

20. From wilting to blooming

To my mother,
My heart was a flower at your feet,
One you had permission to kick,
But you did nothing like it,
Instead you picked it up and planted it somewhere safe,
Where no one could hurt it,
But someone did,
And you saw as the flower wilt,
You still never lost hope in it,
And made it blossom and bloom like it did...

21. The healing

The weight of darkness, a familiar guise,
Had painted shadows in my weary eyes.
A yearning for release, a desperate plea,
To trade this life for sweet oblivion's sea.
Yet, glancing back, a flicker in the gray,
A tapestry of love began to sway.
Warm hands that held me, voices soft and low,
A circle bright, a radiant afterglow.
Through laughter shared and tears that softly fell,
A bond unbreakable, a love I know so well.
A family's embrace, a steadfast, guiding light,
Their unwavering support, a beacon ever bright.
And by my side, a friend, a loyal, steadfast soul,
Who lifts me higher, makes me brave and whole.
With every stumble, every doubt and fear,
Their hand is there, dispelling shadows near.
Though darkness lingers, a whisper in the night,
I see the dawn, a promise shining bright.
For in this tapestry, a lifeline I have found,
In love's embrace, where solace can be found.